LOUGHBOROUGH IN 50 BUILDINGS

LYNNE DYER

I would like to thank all the people of Loughborough for making the town what it is today, and for their interest in its history and development. I would also like to thank my family for their help and support while I've been researching and writing this book.

First published 2018

Amberley Publishing, The Hill, Stroud
Gloucestershire gl5 4EP

www.amberley-books.com

Copyright © Lynne Dyer, 2018

The right of Lynne Dyer to be identified as the Author of this work has been asserted in accordance with the Copyrights, Designs and Patents Act 1988.

Map contains Ordnance Survey data © Crown copyright and database right [2018]

All rights reserved. No part of this book may be reprinted or reproduced or utilised in any form or by any electronic, mechanical or other means, now known or hereafter invented, including photocopying and recording, or in any information storage or retrieval system, without the permission in writing from the Publishers.

British Library Cataloguing in Publication Data.
A catalogue record for this book is available from the British Library.

ISBN 978 1 4456 8093 4 (print)
ISBN 978 1 4456 8094 1 (ebook)

Origination by Amberley Publishing.
Printed in Great Britain.

Contents

Map 4
Key 6
Introduction 7
The 50 Buildings 9

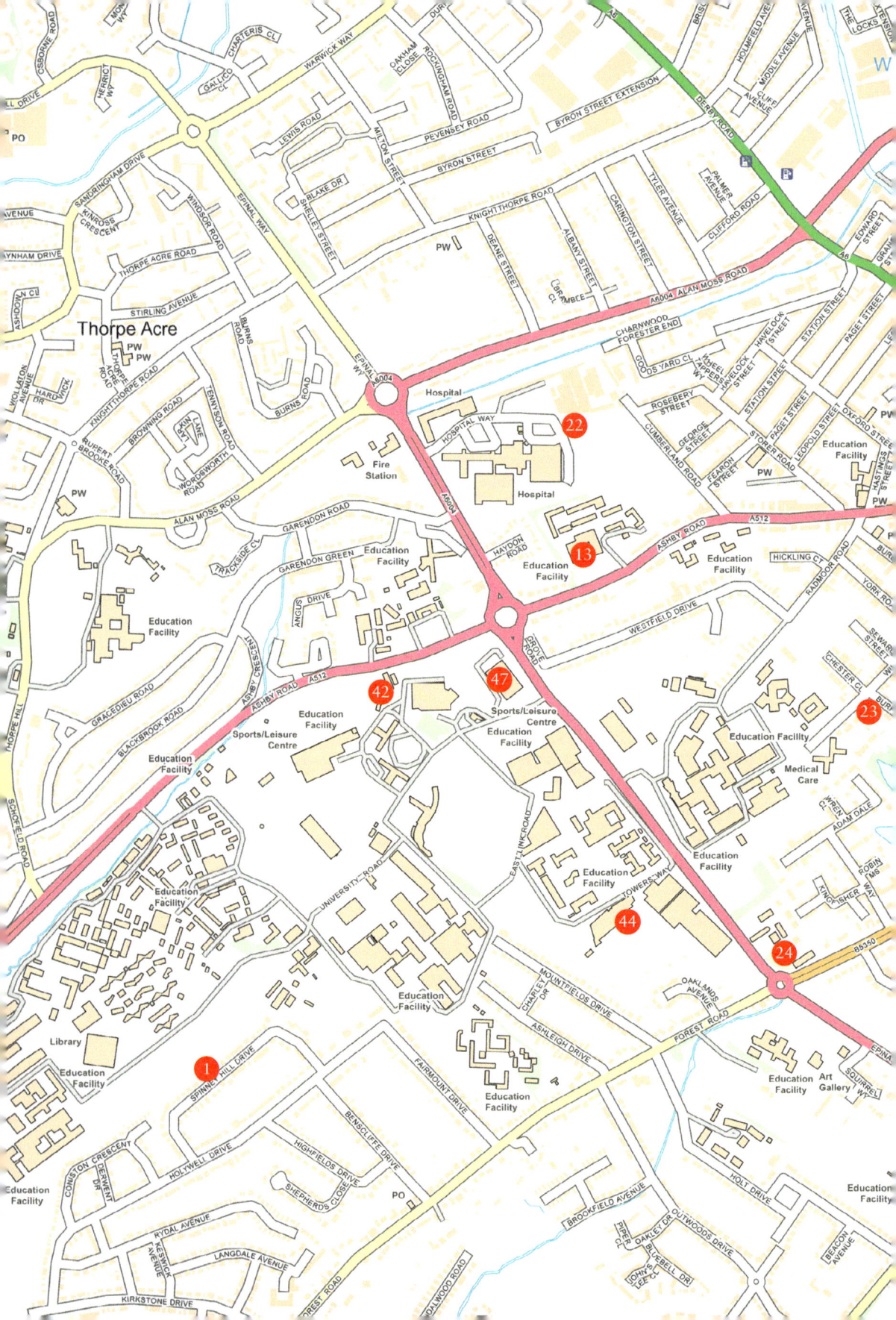

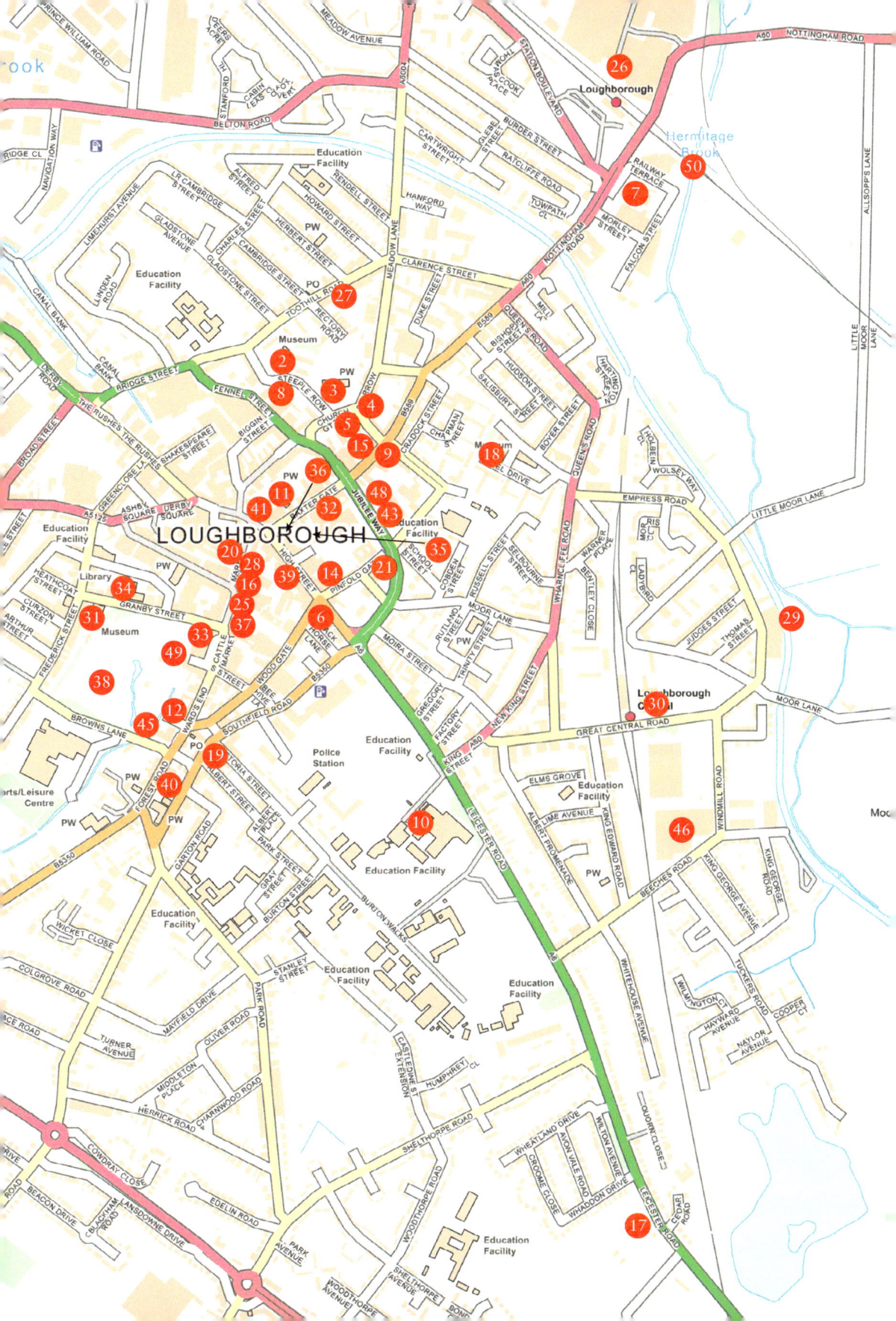

Key

1. Ancient Hill Fort
2. Old Rectory, *c.* 1228
3. Church of All Saints with Holy Trinity, *c.* 1300–1400
4. The Great House, *c.* 1477–1500
5. Manor House, *c.* 1477
6. Organ Grinder, 1781
7. Gainsborough House, *c.* 1800
8. Chesterton House, 1802
9. International Supermarket, 1823
10. White House/Fairfield House, 1823
11. Orange Tree, pre-1828
12. Baxter Gate Baptist Church, 1828
13. The Grove, *c.* 1830
14. Pinfold Gate Cottages, Early/Mid-Nineteenth Century
15. Parks Millwright, 1854
16. Town Hall, 1854
17. Cemetery Chapels, 1856–57
18. Taylors Bell Founders, 1858
19. GTG Engineering, pre-1866
20. Fearon Fountain, 1870
21. Warner School, 1872
22. Messengers, 1877
23. Radmoor House, *c.* 1878
24. The Gables, *c.* 1885
25. NatWest Bank, 1886
26. The Brush, 1889
27. Fearon Hall, 1889
28. HSBC, 1894
29. Herbert Morris, 1897
30. Great Central Railway (GCR), 1898
31. Charnwood Museum, 1898
32. Pizza Express, 1900
33. Temperance Hall, 1900
34. Public Library, 1905
35. Denhams, 1907
36. Lloyds Bank, 1907
37. The Odeon, 1914/1936
38. Loughborough Carillon Tower and War Memorial Museum, 1922–23
39. Poundstretcher, 1930
40. Blacksmith's Arms, 1931
41. *Echo* Offices, 1931
42. Bastard Gates, 1933
43. Beacon Bingo, 1936
44. Towers Hall of Residence, 1964–67
45. John Storer House, 1966
46. Ladybird, 1971
47. Swimming Pool, Loughborough University, 2002
48. Magistrates' Court, 2007
49. Devonshire Square Mural, 2014
50. Bridge to the Future, 2017

Introduction

The scope of this book allows for the inclusion of fifty buildings, each accompanied by a very brief history. Loughborough has two Scheduled Ancient Monuments, one Grade I-, seventy-two Grade II-, and three Grade II*-listed buildings. In addition, a further seventy-three buildings have been Locally Listed by the council for their significance and importance in the development of the town and its people. Choosing just fifty from among these and the vast number of other important and interesting but unlisted buildings was a challenge.

The town's listed buildings are described and documented elsewhere, so although some are included here, many of the buildings covered in this book are neither the most well known, nor the most well documented, and while you may not agree with the selection, it is hoped you will find the choices interesting.

The market town of Loughborough is often overlooked, not just physically from the A60 or the Charnwood Hills, because it sits in the Soar Valley, but because many people are not aware of its existence, nor what it has to offer, nor its history.

According to the entry in the Domesday Book of 1086, Lucteburne, as Loughborough was then known, was large, consisting of thirty-nine households. That there were earlier settlers is evident both from excavated archaeological remains (Roman, although this is scant), and several present-day street names, like Baxter Church and Pinfold Gate – 'Gate' being of Anglo-Saxon origin.

Granted its market charter by Henry III in 1221, in 2017 Loughborough's markets were judged winners in the Best Large Outdoor Market category of the National Association of British Market Authorities (NABMA) competition. Loughborough's annual November street fair, which occupies many of the streets of the town centre including the Market Place, is the last in the travelling season. The original fair charter was also granted in 1221 by Henry III, reaffirmed in 1227 and amended in 1228.

Like many other towns, in the fourteenth century Loughborough was involved in the wool trade, making cloth for use locally and for export, and by the fifteenth century local wool merchant Thomas Burton was working for the Company of the Staple of Calais, the designated market for the export of English wool.

In the centuries that followed, Loughborough, along with many other Leicestershire towns and villages, took up the production of knitted stockings, initially knitting by hand and in the seventeenth century using frames. Restrictions placed on London framework knitters by the London Framework Knitting Company around the turn of the seventeenth century were partly responsible for framework knitters migrating to the Midlands, and Loughborough must surely have benefitted from their expertise.

Until the introduction of sophisticated machinery and diversification into the fashioning of other garments and into lacemaking, framework knitting took place in the home. By the early 1800s the hosiery industry was in the doldrums, and remained stagnant until steam power was introduced to the factories. However, by the mid- to late nineteenth century new industries – particularly iron founding and engineering – were developing, taking advantage of the growing consumer need and export trade, facilitated by transport improvements.

More recently, Loughborough has been the location for a number of pharmaceutical companies – AstraZeneca and 3M – and numerous other industries. The town has benefitted greatly from the growth and popularity of the university, which makes a substantial contribution to both the local and national economy.

To this day, Loughborough has remained a thriving market town, but has also maintained a strong industrial base, being the location for some major companies, like Brush, as well as the UK's sole remaining bell foundry, Taylors.

The stories that are told between the pages of this book are but tiny tales in the history of the town and its buildings, a dearth of buildings in one era and an abundance in another reflecting periods of prosperity and decline. So it is through a discovery of the town's buildings we can begin to piece together a history of Loughborough, a history that can never be complete, for as new information surfaces, so our understanding and knowledge of the town changes with it. This book is but a starting point to discovery.

The 50 Buildings

1. Ancient Hill Fort

Across the UK over 4,000 sites have been identified as either hill forts or possible hill forts. Investigation into sites in the East Midlands has been less well researched than other areas of the UK where there is a greater concentration of known sites. Sites in Leicestershire that have been investigated and positively identified include Beacon Hill, Breedon Hill, Burrough Hill, and Bury Camp; a number of other sites including Life Hill, Robin-a-Tiptoe Hill and Hallaton Wood remain unconfirmed.

According to Loughborough University the institution sits on a former hill fort, and during 2003, the university granted permission to members of the Loughborough Archaeological and Historical Society to undertake an archaeological investigation in the form of a dig. A land survey carried out by the society in 1980 had found some evidence – a large enclosure surrounded by a ditch – but the 2003 event, which was a part of Channel Four's *Time Team Big Dig*, was a chance to dig big.

There is a ditch just visible diagonally across the middle of the photograph.

Although levelled, the land retains a distinct slope.

Aerial photographs of the site taken around 1948 show a double bank enclosed by a ditch, the boundary being marked by a natural curve. However, over the course of many years the land has been levelled, making a positive identification more difficult. The *Big Dig* of 2003 uncovered several sherds of Roman pottery, but little evidence of physical structures.

The university has produced a series of leaflets promoting walks on the campus. Walk Four, The Paddock Walk, takes twenty-five minutes, and the leaflet contains a description and map of the remains of the Iron Age hill fort.

2. Old Rectory, c. 1228

When William John Lyon, rector of Loughborough from 1934 and 1958, moved from Loughborough to Brent Pelham, his successor, Ronald Albert Jones, made the decision not to live in the grand Old Rectory, preferring to live in a smaller new-build. This 'new rectory' was nestled between the Old Rectory and the Church of All Saints. When the Corporation announced they intended to build homes for the elderly on the land surrounding the Old Rectory, the fate of this old building hung in the balance.

The Old Rectory is the oldest of the few remaining stone-built edifices in Loughborough. Although Loughborough had a rector as early as 1193, the earliest written record of the Old Rectory is from 1228, at which time it was owned by the Cortlinstoke family, before being acquired by the church.

By the late Middle Ages the prosperous merchant town of Loughborough provided a substantial residence for its rector and church officials. The grounds contained three barns, stables and pigsties. Pictorial evidence of the Old Rectory is seen in Nichols' *History and Antiquities of Leicestershire* in which the building is presented with four gable ends facing the church, although the artist has not been wholly accurate in the portrayal.

Leicestershire architect Christopher Staveley undertook repairs and improvements to the building around 1800. In 1826 the inside of the building and its roof were destroyed by fire, following which a new frontage, facing onto Rectory Place, was added. During the Victorian period, the extensive gardens were used for fêtes and other fundraising events.

Reaching the end of its life as a home for the local rector, the rectory was saved from complete demolition when the Loughborough Archaeological Society investigated and recorded as much of the building's history as they could establish. By 1967 the majority of the building had been demolished but the medieval core was saved and restored, and now houses a collection of local artefacts, including the cross from the top of Warner School, and an annually changing exhibition.

The remains of the Old Rectory surrounded on two sides by flats.

Above: Close-up of the ancient walls.

Left: Snowfall adds to the appeal of the Old Rectory.

3. Church of All Saints with Holy Trinity, c. 1300–1400

The Church of All Saints with Holy Trinity is the parish church of Loughborough covering Hastings, Lemyngton and Storer wards. It is likely the church is built on the site of a former Norman or Saxon place of worship. Some of the building dates back to around 1330, and the tower was heightened, and a clerestory added in around 1450.

That the church is well positioned on the highest point of the town is indicated by the nearby street names: Toothill Road, from the Saxon word 'tot' meaning a lookout; Sparrow Hill, which means 'little hill'; and Steeple Row, which could be indicative of a steep slope, or may simply be a reference to the church tower itself. Approaching the church from Church Gate (formerly Kirk Gate), the incline is more noticeable.

Originally dedicated to St Peter and St Paul, then to All Saints, but now encompassing the Church of Holy Trinity, this large parish church has undergone various changes over the years, reflecting developments in religious beliefs, in fashion and trends, and in architectural styles. In 1815 Christopher Staveley, who had made earlier repairs to the rectory, made alterations to the church, which included erecting three galleries, and resiting the pulpit.

Subsequent renovations saw the removal of the box pews and gallery, and in the 1860s, while the Revd Henry Fearon was rector, further remodelling was to a plan by the now well-known Sir George Gilbert Scott, who, among other things, rearranged the seating, and enlarged the east window.

The church tower dominating nearby buildings.

Above: The walk up to the church from Fearon Hall.

Left: Renovated First World War memorial.

In the ensuing 100 years, a number of small changes have been made to the church, including a north-side extension, a dedication in the floor of the bell tower to the local bell founders who lost several family members in the First World War, and the creation of a chapel in honour of Thomas Burton, wool merchant and notable benefactor to the town.

Major remodelling around 1960 has been followed over the last fifty years by further works, including renovation of the stonework by David Tarver, a local sculptor. In 2016, work culminated in the renovation and resiting of the magnificent First World War memorial.

4. The Great House, c. 1477–1500

Situated at the junction of Church Gate and Sparrow Hill and occupied by Charles Lowe, a family-run business going back five generations, Nos 37 and 38 and Nos 39 and 40 Church Gate have been variously referred to as the Great House, the Great Hall, the Guildhall and the Lord's Place.

It is believed the buildings date back to the fifteenth century, and, like the Manor House nearby, the timber frame of the buildings have been encased in a brick and stuccoed front, although some timber is exposed inside Nos 37 and 38. Despite many additions and alterations to the buildings, which serve to obscure some of the building's original fabric, it appears that Nos 39 and 40 were constructed following a layout typical of a small medieval house, with a hall and cross passage.

The Great House or Guildhall on the junction of Sparrow Hill and Church Gate.

The rear of the Great House or Guildhall.

During the medieval period, the area around the parish church was the centre of the town. If the buildings were used as a guild hall, this would have been the meeting place for members of the early merchants' guilds. Loughborough had long been active in the wool trade, and Thomas Burton, one of the town's benefactors, who died around 1495, was a wool merchant of the Staple of Calais. Members of the early craft guilds might also have met here, and their workshops may have been situated nearby. The merchant guild would have controlled the purchase of raw wool and the ensuing production and sale of the processed wool, while the craft guilds would have controlled the actual processes of carding, dyeing and weaving.

If the buildings were used by the lord of the manor, in addition to the Manor House, then it is perhaps significant that in 1951, when the boundary wall of the Guildhall was demolished and then rebuilt, the bricks were identified as similar to those used in the building of Kirby Muxloe Castle. The Hastings family, who were the lords of the manor of Loughborough, had built the castle of locally made red brick. When William Hastings died in 1483, the castle was incomplete. His widow continued with the building work for a further year before abandoning it, after which the building suffered from theft of the building material, and the land was used for agriculture. It would be a romantic notion to suggest that perhaps William's son, Edward, used bricks from the castle to build the Guildhall in Loughborough.

The inhabitants of the Great House might at one time have been staff from the Burton Free Grammar School, which was situated in the churchyard opposite, but since the mid-nineteenth century the Lowe family of cabinetmakers, antique dealers and furniture dealers have occupied the building.

The frontage of the Great House or Guildhall.

5. Manor House, c. 1477

Sitting proudly on Sparrow Hill at its junction with the top end of Church Gate, its nineteenth-century white stuccoed frontage creating a dazzling landmark, is the Italian restaurant Caravelli. The restaurateurs have been custodians of this historic building for over five years, but the building's fascinating history goes back much further than this.

The rear of the building has visible post and panel timber framing, and archaeologists have dendro-dated some timbers to around 1477.

During the mid-sixteenth century an extension was built at right angles to the original building, and the attic also probably dates from this time. The east wing was built in the seventeenth century and the frontage partially rebuilt in the late seventeenth or early eighteenth century. During the early nineteenth century, a further brick extension was added to the eastern side, and the building was rendered and the thatched roof replaced by Swithland slate. All these alterations along with the installation of twentieth-century shopfront windows hide the building's real age.

This building was the Manor House, and along with the park, the chapel, the fishponds and the rabbit warrens belonged to the Lord of the Manor of Loughborough. The house was constructed during the time the Hastings family were the lords, 1464–85, after which it passed to the Beaumont family. In 1527 the lordship passed to Thomas Grey, father of Lady Jane Grey, and in 1554 back to the Hastings family, with Sir Edward being created Baron Hastings

Above: The dazzling white frontage of the former Manor House.

Left: The Manor House from the rear.

of Loughborough in 1557. Historians have suggested that Henry Hastings, first Baron Loughborough of Loughborough, and relative of Edward, was born here around 1609.

The manor of Loughborough remained with the Hastings family until 1818 when it is said to have been purchased by Thomas Denning who, upon his death in 1846, left it to Thomas Craddock. However, the Hastings family had sold the Manor House itself as early as 1654, and later it was owned by Thomas Messenger of the local company, Messengers. During the census years of 1841–1901, the house was occupied by a variety of families.

For most of the twentieth century and into the twenty-first century, the premises have had a commercial use, being Putts, a wallpaper and decorating shop (the business latterly situated on Nottingham Road, but closed early 2018, after more than 100 years of trading), an electrical shop, a hairdressing salon and a bike shop. During a period of modernisation around 1950, an ancient fireplace, the weight of which was resting on an oak beam, was found on the first floor, a huge block of stone forming the lintel and side pilasters.

The Manor House has since been converted, first into a hotel, and now Caravelli.

6. Organ Grinder, 1781

In March 1897 the public house known as the Pack Horse, situated in Wood Gate, was auctioned and sold for £3,505. The inside of the substantial premises comprised a bar, tap room, smoke room, back parlour, club room, kitchen, scullery and larder, back kitchen, six bedrooms and a sitting room. Outside buildings included a brewhouse with lofts, sheds, stores and stables catering for thirty-five horses.

The rear of the former Pack Horse.

From the date highlighted on the rear of the building through the use of blue bricks, it would appear the Pack Horse has existed on this site since at least 1781, if not earlier, and at this time it would have been situated on the main London road, which, on its way from Leicester, ran along Pack Horse Lane.

As the name suggests, the Pack Horse would have been a welcome establishment for weary merchant travellers, where they could find food and rest, for themselves and their pack horses.

In 1839, land at the back of the Pack Horse – now a car park – was probably used by Taylors bell founders, when they first arrived in Loughborough to recast the bells of the parish church, before deciding to remain in Loughborough and creating a purpose-built factory site on Freehold Street in 1858.

The Pack Horse was extended along Pack Horse Lane in the nineteenth century, and its original red-brick building was later rendered.

Showing the main entrance on Wood Gate and the brick extension along Pack Horse Lane.

The Pack Horse as The Organ Grinder, part of the Blue Monkey Brewery.

During its life, the establishment has been associated with many breweries including Kimberley Ales (part of the Hardy and Hansons Brewery) and Greene King, and during 1912–38 the then landlord, Harry Sheffield, brewed his own beer, using water from an underground spring in the pub's stables.

In 2012, the Pack Horse was bought by the Nottingham-based Blue Monkey Brewery, a brewery named after the nickname given to the blue flames that used to rise from the ironworks in nearby Stanton. Renamed The Organ Grinder, in 2013 the pub won the Campaign for Real Ale (CAMRA) Pub of the Year award for the Loughborough and north-west Leicestershire district.

7. Gainsborough House, c. 1800

It is not easy to establish the construction date of Gainsborough House; the Borough Council listing suggests this may be an early nineteenth-century property, possibly with an earlier core. There are other buildings in Loughborough with older inner cores, some exposed – the Old Rectory – some hidden behind a modern façade – No. 54 Church Gate – and others demolished – the former Irish shop, also on Church Gate.

The beautiful property, with its fresh-looking, white-painted rendering and green-painted window frames, has a Swithland slate roof and a porch contained within pillars, but now sits uncomfortably surrounded by industrial properties and the Civic Amenities site. In 1890, the grounds in which this house was situated were more substantial, but with the proposed new railway of the Manchester, Sheffield & Lincolnshire Railway Co. (the MS&LR, later to become the Great Central Railway (GCR)), Thomas Tyler's horse dealing business lost some of its ground, as did the Brush Electrical Engineering Co. and gardens belonging to several prominent local industrialists.

Gainsborough House is now adorned with a Leicestershire Green Plaque commemorating the life of Sunloch, the local horse that won the 1914 Grand National.

Above: Gainsborough House at the busy Nottingham Road junction.

Left: Detail of the Leicestershire Green Plaque awarded to Sunloch, the steeplechaser.

8. Chesterton House, 1802

Rectory Place, the tiny pedestrianised walkway leading from Fennel Street – now part of the town's inner relief road – to the leafy junction of Steeple Row and the longer Rectory Place, is aptly named as is the view from Fennel Street along this walkway of the Old Rectory.

Built in 1802 for local hosier Thomas Barfoot Oliver, whose manufactory was at one time on Mill Street (now Market Street), the house is an impressive and imposing four storeys, part of a group of three properties, and has recently been refurbished.

The plaque adorning the front of this Georgian building tells of the building's importance: in 1850 it was here that the first girls' grammar school in the country began. Headmistress Miss Ellen Charnock came from a seminary in Bootham, bringing with her four or five boarders who wished to finish their education under her tutelage.

The school was successful, but the building began to suffer through lack of funds to maintain it, and eventually it relocated to the grammar school on Leicester Road. The building passed through the hands of Woolley, a local land agent and surveyor, and Warner, a local hosier, and has been occupied by the Chesterton House Group since 1991.

Chesterton House on the left.

9. International Supermarket, 1823

Constructed in 1823, the International Supermarket on Sparrow Hill has had many functions over the years. Originally this was a purpose-built theatre managed by a Mr Bennett, who also managed theatres in Ashby, Coventry, Wolverhampton and Worcester. Local subscribers paid £700 for the building, which opened with two plays: *Speed the Plough* by Morton and *Warlock of the Glen* by Walker.

However, the theatre was not a huge success, and regular performances dwindled until 1830 when there was a revival, led by performances by Master B. Grossmith. So successful was this revival that gas lighting was installed in the theatre in 1845. This revival was short-lived: in 1848 the theatre was sold and after conversion works, reopened as a church, although it was not long before this was remodelled and a first floor inserted for use as a dance hall and music salon.

Following its sale to the Loyal Sovereign Lodge of Oddfellows, the building became known as the Oddfellows Hall, and was used continuously as their meeting place, as well as for occasional theatrical performances, dancing and dance lessons, and was one of the earliest venues to show films.

In 1945, Messrs Adkinson and Freckelton used the building as an auction mart to complement their business on Leicester Road. By 1962 the building had become a cycle repair shop run by the Hubbards, and has since been in use by various retailers, including Cunningham's Carpets, Up the Mountain, and today it is the International Supermarket.

The former theatre, now the International Supermarket.

The windowless building in the foreground shows the length of the theatre. The tiny spire in the middle of the picture is the one on the front of the building.

Locally listed by Charnwood Borough Council, the building is comparable with the Georgian Theatre Royal in Richmond, which, although built a few years earlier in 1788, is of a very similar design, having been restored to its former glory, and shows regular productions during the season.

10. White House/Fairfield House, 1823

The firm of Paget and White, worsted spinners, was created around 1792, and was certainly well established by 1807. Such was the success of the company that by 1823 William White, a partner in the business, which also operated a corn mill at nearby Zouch, was living with his family in Fairfield House, a substantial property in a pleasant setting close to the Leicester road.

William died in 1849, and the Pagets left the company; Arthur Paget set up his own engineering company focused on producing textile machinery. Meanwhile, William White's family and descendants continued to live in Fairfield House. His sons, Frank and William Edward, continued to run the company, which was then called F. and W. E. White. Their hosiery manufacturing business was based in nearby Wood Gate and Beehive Lane.

When William Edward White died in 1893, Fairfield House passed into the hands of Augusta Sophia Middleton, the widow of the local banker Edward William Craddock

Middleton. Edward, son of Edward Chatterton Middleton, was brought up at The Grove on Ashby Road, and on marrying Augusta moved with her to Shelthorpe Cottage (now the Cedars Hotel), where Augusta continued to live for a number of years after his death, before moving down the road to Fairfield House. Right up until her own death in 1922, Augusta was active in local society, attending garden parties, fêtes, and other important local events.

Around 1852 the Loughborough Grammar School moved from its premises near the parish church to a site very close to Fairfield House. The first buildings to be constructed were the 'Big School' and the 'School House', and in 1879 the Grammar School was joined by the Loughborough High School, which transferred from its premises in Chesterton House and became the Loughborough Endowed Schools.

Following the death of Augusta Middleton, it was only a matter of time before Fairfield House was acquired by the Endowed Schools, it being so close to the school, and Fairfield Preparatory School was created in 1929. Today the modified and extended house provides a focal point for the pupils of the preparatory school.

The White House viewed from Southfields Park.

The White House viewed from Leicester Road.

11. Orange Tree, pre-1828

The earliest reference to the Wheatsheaf pub in Ward's End is in the 1828 Pigot's Directory, when J. Murfin was the landlord. In the nineteenth century many towns had yards and courts, accessed via a doorway or arch, and Loughborough was no different. Yards with a large carriageway arch usually led to workshops behind, like the one at Parks Millwrights, but where there was a smaller doorway, often called a court, this usually led to a group of houses that faced into a courtyard.

Next to the Wheatsheaf was a doorway with a nameplate above saying 'Court C', which led to a number of properties clustered around a courtyard. On the 1851 census return, Henry Moore is one of the inhabitants of a property in this courtyard. Like many people of the time, he is working from home, in his case, making spar ornaments, fashioned from Derbyshire alabaster, most likely to sell in seaside resorts like Skegness.

At some point the Wheatsheaf became associated with Offilers, the Derby brewery, which was originally created as Vine Brewery in 1876, and renamed Offilers in 1892. This popular Loughborough pub was taken over by the Orange Tree chain in 1998 and is still thriving. In recent years it has had several refurbishments, the latest being in 2017, when sadly, the historic sign above the courtyard door was lost.

The Orange Tree group also runs the pub next door, The Kelso, which had previously been known as The News Room pub, and prior to that GT News and Scoggins.

The Orange Tree pub pictured in 2014.

12. Baxter Gate Baptist Church, 1828

Constructed in 1828, the Baxter Gate Baptist Church provided accommodation for the burgeoning congregation and Sunday school attendees, and complemented the existing Baptist church on Wood Gate built in 1792. The latter was demolished and rebuilt, reopening in 1882 and extended again in 1904, between which times, in 1898, a further Baptist church opened on King Street.

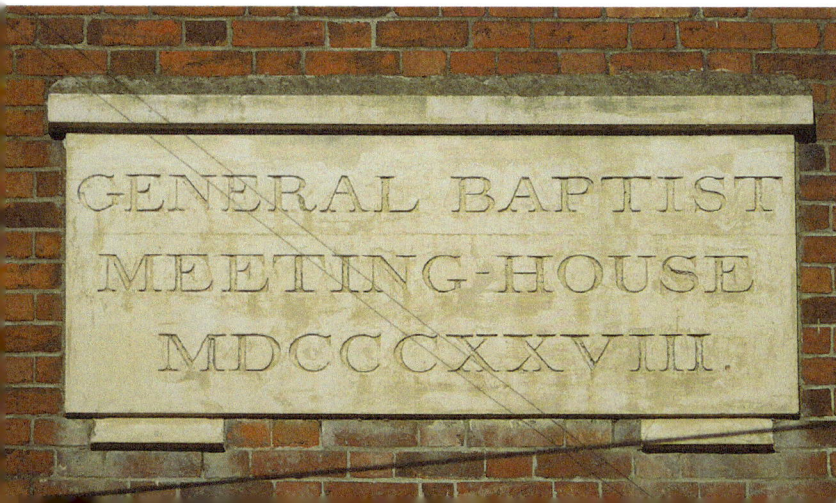

The inscribed tablet showing the construction date of 1828.

Above: The church set back from the roadside.

Right: One of the war memorials at the Baptist church.

Although set back from the roadside today, before the street widening of the late 1920s/early 1930s the Baxter Gate Baptist Church was positioned even further behind the line of the earlier buildings. There have been several amendments and additions to the building including new Sunday school buildings in 1846, a lecture theatre in 1865, more schoolrooms in 1883 and a new hall with rooms upstairs in 1896, followed by extensions to the porch.

For more than seventy years, the three Baptist churches flourished, but it was decided to unite the congregations of all three, and the first such meeting took place at the Baxter Gate church in 1973. Demolition of the Wood Gate premises began in early 1976, and of the King Street church in April of the same year. However, the Sunday school building attached to the King Street chapel passed into the hands of the Islamic Community Cultural Association, and today it remains an active place of worship.

The Baxter Gate church continues to thrive and is a quiet sanctuary in the hustle and bustle of the newly developed Baxter Gate leisure area.

13. The Grove, c. 1830

The houses that adorn Ashby Road are predominantly substantial Victorian homes constructed of local red Tucker's brick. Many of these were designed by the Loughborough architect Barrowcliff and built by William Moss of Loughborough. One of the few surviving properties from a slightly earlier period, around 1830, is The Grove. Set back somewhat from the road, rather than displaying its construction, The Grove is rendered and painted white.

The Grove set back in its own grounds.

Early occupants were the Middletons, a family of Loughborough bankers, based in the town since 1790. When in 1848 the Revd Robert James Bunch arrived to be rector of the recently created Emmanuel Church, the Middletons moved to Market Place, perhaps above their banking business, and Revd Bunch moved into The Grove.

It is not clear if the Emmanuel vicarage existed at this time, but certainly by 1857 Revd Bunch was now living at the vicarage (now the Forest Court university halls of residence), and the Middletons had moved back to The Grove.

Edward Chatterton Middleton died a couple of months after his wife, in 1878, and by 1881 Edward Parkinson White, a manufacturer of merino wool, and his family had moved into the property. When Edward died in 1887, the solicitor William Frederick Beardsley and his family made The Grove their home. William died in 1914 and his wife in 1923.

When The Grove came up for sale in 1923 Loughborough College were interested in purchasing it as accommodation for its growing number of students. To help raise funds the college organised a bazaar and Christmas fête, which was held in the Town Hall over a four-day period in the days preceding Christmas. Such was the variety of stalls and amusements that the event raised over £2,000, which helped the college to purchase the property in 1924. After some alterations were made, The Grove began its long life as student accommodation.

Today, The Grove forms part of the Harry French complex of university student accommodation and is a Grade II-listed building.

The Grove visible in the winter landscape.

The Grove detail of the stone pillars.

14. Pinfold Gate Cottages, Early/Mid-Nineteenth Century

A local estate agent recently (February 2017) described one of the group of ten terraced cottages on Pinfold Gate as being of 'national historic importance'. Whether or not this is an example of estate agent hyperbole is less important than the fact that this row of cottages is of historic importance to Loughborough.

Along Pinfold Gate are a number of old properties and among these were workshops used by framework knitters and lacemakers. These cottages were built as homes for these and other workers, like those from William Cotton's powered knitting machine factory, which opened in the 1870s and backed onto the cottages.

More recently a doctors' surgery has been built adjacent to the cottages, and the rear land, which used to abut the hospital, was used as a car park. Today, the land to the rear is still used as a car park, but the hospital has been replaced with a new leisure complex that houses a multiplex cinema, with a frontage onto Baxter Gate. Despite the new inner relief road changing the outlook of the cottages, as parking is now allowed directly in front of them, the cottages retain their charm and importance to the town.

Some of the cottages on Pinfold Gate.

15. Parks Millwright, 1854

Situated near the heart of the old town is a terrace of three mid-nineteenth-century houses, the end one of which has a carriageway arch over which is a date stone inscribed 'Parks Millwrights 1854'.

The exact nature of the work of this millwright is not known but given the proximity of the business to hosiery and knitting factories on Nottingham Road, and later Cottons on Baxter Gate, it is likely that William Park's business was concerned with the production and maintenance of textile mill machinery. Or, given its proximity to the Upper and Lower mills at Cotes, it could be associated with corn mills.

In the years when mills were vital to the processing of grains, the millwright would have been a skilled joiner, able to fashion and mend wooden machinery parts. Once Britain became more industrialised the millwright's skills would be in metalwork.

Through the archway is a workshop, also constructed in 1854, which until recently was still in use as a motorcycle maintenance workshop.

Left: The inscribed date stone above Parks Millwrights.

Below: The terrace of Victorian houses showing Parks Millwrights on the left.

16. Town Hall, 1854

It has been suggested that realising there was no suitable place to hold public meetings and events, a number of local tradesmen met at a bank in Market Place to consider the problem. The result of their deliberations was the formation of a public company, and the pledge of donations from many local dignitaries. Eventually, fifty-five donations totalling approximately £8,000 were made, and the foundation stone for the Corn Exchange, designed by Walter Slater, was laid in October 1854, the building being completed in 1855.

While the corn exchange hall, where local farmers met to trade, was available for public events and entertainment, the lavishly decorated Victoria Rooms, on the upper floor, were reserved for balls.

Following the incorporation of the borough in 1888, the town council, looking for suitable premises for their administrative functions, bought the building from the Corn Exchange Company for £5,000. Renovation work, including redecoration of the Victoria Rooms at a cost of £56 10s, the addition of a parlour for the mayor and a chamber for the council, and a strong room costing £155, added a further £3,000 to the overall cost. The building was renamed as the Town Hall, and a new clock was donated by Edward Basil Farnham, a former MP.

In May 1890 the mayor, Alderman Griggs, spoke to the General Purposes Committee expressing the desire to replace the internal gas lights with electric ones. The town clerk had already written to the Brush Electrical Engineering Co. enquiring about the likely cost, but the meeting did not reach an agreement, so electric lighting was not installed until a later date.

Today the magnificent Town Hall building sits in a prominent position on the edge of the Market Place, and presents a stunning view from the end of Market Street. The ground floor houses the Sock Gallery, in which there are regularly changing art exhibitions, and the theatre has regular shows throughout the year. The Victoria Rooms are opened for special events – the hall can be hired for weddings – and the Town Hall still performs its civic functions.

The Town Hall.

The Town Hall showing the bellcote.

17. Cemetery Chapels, 1856–57

The government's first Public Health Act (1848), which permitted the creation of local Boards of Health, received royal assent following a second national outbreak of cholera. A series of Burial Acts were also passed, culminating in the Burial Act 1854, allowing town councils to create Burial Boards, such boards being responsible for establishing parish cemeteries.

Loughborough Cemetery was created following the passing of the Burial Acts, the chapel being designed by architects Bellamy and Hardy of Lincoln in the popular Gothic Revival style, and built by John Sudbury of Loughborough.

At a ceremony in July 1856, a procession of members of the Burial Board, which comprised many well-known local men, including Edward Chatterton Middleton, Edward Warner, Beauvoir Brock, and Henry Toone, walked from the Town Hall to the cemetery, where Edward Middleton laid the foundation stone for the chapels.

Expansion at the end of the nineteenth century was followed by the creation of a new cemetery in 1947, and in 2017 further expansion has been proposed. Remedial and conversion work was carried out on the deteriorating chapels in 1993 and they are now home to the Cibes Lift Group.

According to Pevsner these are the best cemetery chapels in the country.

Above: The cemetery chapels viewed from the Leicester Road entrance.

Right: Cemetery chapel detail.

18. Taylors Bell Founders, 1858

The Taylor family have been involved in bell founding since Robert Taylor was apprenticed to Edward Arnold in St Neots, an apprenticeship he completed in 1782. When Arnold moved to Leicester two years later, Robert was left in charge of the St Neots foundry, and by 1821 was such an experienced maker that he created a foundry at Oxford.

Car park of the Pack Horse, the probable site of the original bell foundry.

Robert's eldest son, William, entered the family business, making bells until his death in 1854. Robert's younger son, John, also joined the family business in Oxford, but in 1839 was lured away to Loughborough to recast the bells of the parish church. He set up this branch of the business in Pack Horse Lane, probably in the yard at the back of the Pack Horse pub.

When John Taylor died in 1858, his eldest son, John William Taylor, carried on the bell-founding tradition with his brother Pryce. In 1858, land was purchased in Loughborough to build a new foundry, on Chapman Street and Freehold Street, which included a carillon tower. The foundry buildings were altered and added to in 1898 by local architects Barrowcliff and Allcock.

For some time after Pryce's early death at the age of twenty-seven, John William worked on his own until his son, also John William, was old enough to join the family firm. It was John William Jr who travelled to London and took the order for the Great Paul bell for St Paul's Cathedral, the cast of which is now on display in Queen's Park, Loughborough.

Taylors Bell Founders have been responsible for casting church bells throughout the UK and beyond. In 1923, they cast the bells for the Loughborough Carillon, each of the forty-seven bells being inscribed with a memorial, and the largest bell being dedicated to members of the Taylor family who died during the First World War. Brass memorial plaques to the family can also be found in the base of the parish church tower.

The bell foundry buildings are beginning to show signs of age: the company has recently bid for funding from a variety of sources to complete an extensive renovation, to include a state-of-the-art museum facility and suitable storage facilities for the extensive archival material the company holds.

Above: The extensive bell foundry buildings.

Right: Part of the Victorian factory.

19. GTG Engineering, pre-1866

The GTG Engineering Company works with the aerospace and allied industries, providing mechanical testing, precision engineering, metal specimens and equipment. Their business premises are prominently situated at the end of a residential street, near the town centre.

GTG Engineering have occupied these premises since 1959 when the company was established, having taken over the building from the Bentley Engineering Group who, in the early 1950s, had acquired the firm of D. Grudgings & Sons, a needle-making factory situated in this building.

Grudgings, needle makers, was founded around 1850, and originally had premises in nearby Wood Gate. At the time, much of the trade in Loughborough was based around the hosiery manufacturing industry, and the bearded needles made by Grudgings were in high demand for use with the innovative machinery of Paget, and later William Cotton. So successful was Grudgings' needle-making business that it expanded and a new factory was opened in School Street, followed in around 1866 by another in Albert Street.

The Albert Street works was the smallest of the premises. Developments in needle making were predominantly made at the School Street works, where they began to manufacture more modern latch needles and parts for knitting frames.

During the First World War, when imports of German-made needles were unavailable, the Grudgings factories thrived. However, by the early 1950s the company had been bought out.

The two-storey part of GTG Engineering from Albert Street.

Above: GTG Engineering fronting onto Albert Street.

Below: Rear and side of GTG Engineering at the junction of Bedford Street and Royland Road.

20. Fearon Fountain, 1870

During the 1800s, Loughborough, like other places, suffered outbreaks of cholera. It was probably the outbreak of 1848, leading to a death rate of around twenty-eight per thousand, that spurred on the new rector of Loughborough, Henry Fearon, to campaign for a clean water supply for the people of the town.

Having studied sanitary science, Fearon was aware of the impact of drinking from a contaminated water supply, and when an inquest into the cholera outbreak, headed by William Lee, was heard, Fearon's argument was persuasive.

Responsible for maintaining cleanliness through the town, the Board of Guardians appointed under the Poor Law Act in 1834 were unable to cope with the cholera outbreak, so a Town Board of Health was elected. This board agreed upon the need for a clean water supply and appeared to make some provisions, a drainage system being in place by 1855. However, the water supply was not available until 1870, when the reservoir at Nanpantan was completed.

In celebration of this new piped water supply, Fearon commissioned a Gothic-style drinking fountain to be placed in the market square, unveiled at a ceremony attended by thousands of townsfolk.

The fountain still stands today, having been renovated in 1981 by local sculptor David Tarver and rededicated in 2014.

The Fearon Fountain celebrating Loughborough's first piped water supply.

A plaque on the Fearon Fountain celebrating the renovations of 1981.

Detail of the Fearon Fountain.

21. Warner School, 1872

One of very few remaining stone-built buildings in Loughborough, Warner School (also known as Warner Street, or Warner C of E School) stands proudly on the edge of the inner relief road, which was opened in 2014. However, it wasn't always like this...

Built in 1872, the school was placed on land given by Edward Warner, who also paid for its construction. The Warner family were involved in taking the local hosiery industry forward with innovative practices, and lived in some of the most prestigious houses in the area. Not only did the Warners provide the school, they also provided accommodation for the headteacher in an adjoining house.

Warner School before demolition, with the headteacher's house to the right.

Initially closely associated with the Church of All Saints, when the church of Holy Trinity was built in 1878, this also became closely connected with the school. The school opened as a mixed school for infants and a through girls' school, for ages seven to fourteen, and was built to accommodate 255 children.

The fabric of the school changed little over time, but the pupils did. In 1923, the junior pupils went on to Emmanuel School, but in 1931 this changed, the juniors staying at Warner and the senior girls moving on to Limehurst, which had recently been completed. At the time of its closure in 1989, Warner School was a voluntary-aided Church of England school.

Two years later, in 1991, the school reopened as Pinfold Gate Day Nursery. This successful enterprise ended with the coming of the inner relief road when the main school building was demolished, leaving only the lonely remains of the headteacher's house, which has now been adapted as private accommodation.

Above: Headteacher's house of Warner's School viewed from Jubilee Way.

Below: Headteacher's house of Warner's School viewed from Pinfold Gate. (Credit: Thomas Dyer-Hill).

22. Messengers, 1877

As early as 1855 plumber, glazier and glass-fitter Thomas Goode Messenger had business premises on High Street, behind which was situated the former Wood Gate Magistrates' Court. In 1858 he registered the company under the name Messenger & Co. William White, in his *Gazetteer* of 1863, describes the company as a plumbers and hydraulic engineers.

In 1874, the company passed to the ownership of Walter Chapman Burder, and soon the manufacturing part of the business was moved to Cumberland Road, while the administrative work remained on High Street. In 1895, the Cumberland Road premises was extended and the administrative function moved there from High Street. Could the decision to move to this area have been influenced by the proximity of the Charnwood Forest Railway, which made the transportation of the firm's products easier?

The rows of Victorian houses – small terraced ones, and larger gentlemen's residences – built around the Messengers works in Cumberland Road, were affectionately referred to as the 'Messengers village' and it was here that both workers and managers lived.

Field House on Ashby Road was built in 1887 for Burder himself, who lived there until his death in 1931. During his involvement in the company, the business evolved into horticultural builders and hot water apparatus manufacturers, and a foundry was built on the Cumberland Road site. Messenger catalogues advertise glass, green-, summer and peach houses, verandas, vineries and fruit frames, as well as boilers and heating systems. With their comprehensive offering, Messengers captured the market.

The Messenger factory viewed from Hospital Walk.

Right: The ghost of the Messenger iron foundry.

Below: Part of the Victorian Messenger factory buildings.

23. Radmoor House, c. 1878

A small student hall of residence in an old house, close to Loughborough College, this traditional Victorian detached house was once home to some of Loughborough's notable industrialists and the birthplace of many of Loughborough's inhabitants.

Built around 1878, close to the more substantial Burleigh Fields House, Radmoor House was home to Arthur Paget, a manufacturer of knitting, weaving and textile machinery, inventor of a cricket scoring board and whose innovative steam-powered hosiery knitting machines were exhibited in 1889 at the Paris Exposition. Arthur lived with his wife Rose, their eight children and five servants.

After Arthur died in 1895 Rose moved away, and the extensive grounds of Radmoor House were given over to a new children's playground, separated from the house by an oak fence. By 1911 the house was occupied by Ernest Edwin Coltman, son of Huram Coltman, of H. Coltman & Sons, boilermakers. Ernest and his wife lived at Radmoor until their respective deaths in 1934 and 1936.

In January 1937 newspaper advertisements appeared appealing for staff for a new nursing home, and by 1938 this was established at Radmoor House. Later, Radmoor became a popular place for mothers to give birth, before finally closing in 1969.

From 1970 onwards, Radmoor House became accommodation for students of Loughborough College. During its first year as such, the large first-floor room, with

Radmoor House viewed from Radmoor Road with its bay window facing the park.

Above: Single-storey outbuildings at Radmoor, 2013.

Below: The extended outbuildings providing further student accommodation.

easy-clean linoleum flooring, was unoccupied and known as the Operating Theatre. Some students shared ghost tales they'd heard of a young girl sobbing on the stairs – perhaps related to the house's days as a nursing home.

Still student accommodation today, the outbuildings/coach house were demolished in 2015 and rebuilt as student flats and the garden has been recently tidied up and cleared.

Despite its conversion from family home to nursing home, and then to student accommodation, Radmoor House retains its unique charm and enviable location next to the recreation ground. Little 'jitties' criss-crossing the area lead to Ashby Road and the town centre, the most appealingly named of which is True Lovers Walk!

24. The Gables, c. 1885

There are several large houses in Loughborough – The Elms and the White House are examples – but none so striking as The Gables, which occupies a prominent position at the junction of Forest Road and Epinal Way.

Built around 1885, The Gables was home to the Clarke family, who owned a very successful dyeing company, which was established in 1825 and was situated facing

The Gables viewed from Epinal Way.

Devonshire Square, extending into what is now known as Old Bleach Yard and the Granby Street car park. It is believed that William Clarke, while living on Forest Road, commissioned the building of The Gables as a home for him and his family, where the living conditions would be beneficial for one of his daughters who is thought to have had asthma.

After William died in 1905, his wife moved away from The Gables to a substantial Victorian semi-detached house nearby, once owned by Thomas Messenger, the founder of the local firm Messengers, and The Gables was bought by local solicitor Richard Sutton Clifford. Clifford had recently been mayor of the borough and ran his offices from No. 19 Baxter Gate, which was also the offices of A. E. King, architects, whom he employed to improve The Gables by adding heating to the outbuildings. The boiler for the heating system in the house itself was replaced later, in 1922.

The Gables remained in the hands of Clifford until his death in 1939. By the mid-1940s it was owned by The Brush, and used as accommodation for their apprentices, and by the late 1970s The Gables was a hall of residence for Loughborough University of Technology, before passing to Loughborough College. A sympathetic renovation of the house by ISG Construction, which included the demolition of two outbuildings, was carried out in 2012 to a design by Marcini Curran. The hall, along with an adjacent new development called White Flats, is now accommodation for athletes, forming part of the Elite Athlete Performance Centre.

The Gables viewed from Forest Road, with the White Flats peeking out on the right.

25. NatWest Bank, 1886

The prolific Nottingham-born architect Watson Fothergill was responsible for the design of the building on Cattle Market now occupied by the NatWest Bank. The Nottingham and Nottinghamshire Banking Co., for whom this building was originally created in 1886, was established as early as 1834 in Nottingham, and quickly grew, opening new branches around the area, including one in Loughborough in 1834, on High Street, and later one in Market Place.

The new premises on Cattle Market was designed by Watson Fothergill during a time when his style was developing from Gothic Revival to Old English Revival. This particular bank, very like the one he designed at Newark, still uses some Gothic motifs – for example the shield between the first-floor windows – but it is clear that Fothergill's style was changing.

Like several other buildings in the town centre, what is now the NatWest is constructed of red brick and uses terracotta for decoration. It was built by local firm Needhams, and has a date of 1886 – the date of completion – on the date stone, the building opening for business in early 1887.

The NatWest Bank designed by Nottingham architect Watson Fothergill.

Detail of a Gothic motif on the NatWest Bank.

26. The Brush, 1889

Affectionately known by the locals as 'The Brush', the Anglo-American Brush Electric Light Corporation began in London in 1879, focussed on the production of dynamos, arc lamps and incandescent bulbs. Although the new electricity industry was burgeoning, development was hampered by the introduction of the [UK] Electric Lighting Act (1882), which placed restrictions on the provision of electricity.

This was superseded by the Act of 1888, and Brush began to outgrow its London base, so the operation moved to Loughborough. In 1889, Brush amalgamated with the Falcon

Part of the Brush factory buildings.

Engine and Car Works, set up by Henry Hughes in 1882, with a £60,000 investment. Henry Hughes & Co., created in 1857, originally built wagons and horse-drawn tramcars, before becoming Hughes's Locomotive and Tramway Engine Works in 1877, when he split from his business partner Huram Coltman, and then the Falcon Engine and Car Works in 1882.

One of the first things the Brush company did when it arrived from London was reply to the local council with a quote for the probable cost of replacing the gas lighting in the Town Hall with electric lighting.

As the business of Brush has changed over the years – Brush Coachworks, Brush Electrical Machines, Brush Switchgear, Brush Traction – so the company has acquired and built new buildings on its site: in 1907 it leased the British Automobile Development Co. buildings, and around 1920 it built the turbine shop.

If the Herbert Morris factory provides the boatman with a view of a building 'lacking in architectural merit,' anyone arriving in Loughborough on the London–Midland mainline train is greeted by the architecturally impressive Brush turbine shop, and if one arrives by night, the illuminated signs are reminiscent of the bright lights of Piccadilly Circus.

The Brush factory viewed from the Midland Mainline railway.

The illuminations at the Brush.

27. Fearon Hall, 1889

Standing adjacent to the churchyard of All Saints with Holy Trinity, and close to the Old Rectory, Fearon Hall is an impressive Victorian Gothic Revival red-brick building. Its very name hints at its importance to the area, for Henry Fearon was the rector of Loughborough from 1848 to 1885, becoming Archdeacon of Leicester in 1863, and Fearon Hall was created as a memorial to him.

Fearon Hall viewed from the parish church.

The original design for the Sunday school accommodation and the memorial hall was by George Hodson. Land identified for use was part of the Glebelands, and money to construct the building was raised through a Fearon Memorial Fund and various fundraising activities, including a grand oriental bazaar held in the grounds of the grammar school on Burton Walks.

Sufficient funds were quickly raised and the Fearon Hall, constructed by Mr Needham, was opened on Wednesday 1 May 1889. With a 26-foot frontage onto Rectory Place, the building comprised the Sunday school rooms on the ground floor with the memorial hall taking up the whole of the upstairs, being a massive 80 feet 6 inches long and 30 feet 9 inches wide. The creation of the Sunday school and memorial hall was part of a wider building and improvement programme, which also saw the bells of the church rehung and the repair of one of the church piers.

However, with the original building design too expensive to complete, a temporary frontage was constructed until a more permanent one could be afforded. Around ten years after the building was opened, the temporary frontage was made permanent and an external staircase added. Further improvement work took place and the building was extended in around 1910.

Over the years Fearon Hall has been used by the local community for many regular and one-off events including Scout groups, bazaars and fêtes, a meeting place for the Ruri-Decanal Association, a concert venue, a venue for industrial exhibitions, and much more.

Today, with a strapline 'The urban village hall in the heart of Loughborough', Fearon Hall is a thriving community centre and has recently benefitted from structural improvements.

'The urban village hall in the heart of Loughborough'.

28. HSBC, 1894

The banking company of Middleton and partners moved from the Wharf to Market Place in 1797. Under the care of Edward Chatterton Middleton, the premises became an important local landmark, the building itself having verandas adorned with flowers and plants tended by Edward who was a keen horticulturalist.

At his death in 1878 there followed a crisis in the bank that led to its closure, the business and building being taken over by the Leicestershire Banking Co. In a matter of about twenty years, the building was deemed no longer suitable for its purpose, so architects were commissioned to design a new one, and it is this building that still stands in Market Place today.

The chosen architects, Goddard, Paget and Goddard, were a well-established Leicester firm, who had designed houses, stables, churches and a number of local branch buildings for the Leicestershire Banking Co. Their design for the Loughborough branch was built by Loughborough builders Moss, and is very striking, being built to an early sixteenth-century French Renaissance-style design, beautifully complemented by being sited adjacent to the imposing Italianate Town Hall.

Standing on a plinth of polished red granite, the front of the Loughborough bank building is of Portland stone. The banking hall and banking offices were situated at ground-floor level, while upstairs originally housed private offices and a residence for the caretaker. Today, the banking

Contemporary hanging baskets on the new bank building.

hall has been opened up as one vast space filled with machines, while the upstairs has cashiers working behind a traditional bank counter. The pilasters framing the entrance to the bank bear the date 1893, the date of commencement of construction of the new building.

That there has been a bank situated on this plot for over 200 years is quite an achievement, and the current building will be celebrating its 125th anniversary in 2019.

Left: Pilaster bearing the date of construction of what is now the HSBC.

Below: The upper floors of the HSBC building.

29. Herbert Morris, 1897

Herbert Morris and Frank Bastert founded their lifting pulley blocks works in 1884 in Sheffield, moving the company to Empress Road, Loughborough, in 1897. This impressive building sits alongside the Grand Union Canal, and has a distinctive, rather appealing style, described by Historic England as 'singularly lacking in architectural merit and entirely functional in appearance'.

The factory buildings spread along and across Empress Road north and south, and by 1908 the works had its own power station providing electricity. In 1911, Morris and Bastert parted company but the firm continued, and for many years Herbert Morris Cranes was a major engineering company in the East Midlands, manufacturing electric, pneumatic and hand overhead travelling cranes, conveyors, lifting gear and similar, and at its height employing over 2,000 staff.

In 1916 the Empress Works, as it was known, was one of the early adopters of the electric light bulb. Unfortunately, in January of that year, as the electric light shone through the glass roof of the works, it attracted the attention of a passing Zeppelin airship with disastrous and fatal consequences. Nonetheless, the business went from strength to strength. In 1920, it took over the business of Huram Coltman, makers of steam engines, boilers and a 20-hp car, and in 1932 the electric crane and switch-gear business of F. H. Royce, who was a partner in the Rolls-Royce car production company.

The Herbert Morris factory spreading along Empress Road.

The Herbert Morris factory viewed from the Grand Union Canal.

In 1959, the company took over British MonoRail, and by 1975 had other subsidiaries including Linear Motors and Crane Aid Services. In 1977, Morris was acquired by Davy International.

Herbert Morris died in 1931, his company being described in his obituary as one of the biggest in the world devoted solely to the manufacture of lifting machinery, and he, despite his quiet, private nature, is considered to be one of the greatest industrialists of the time.

Some of the factory on Empress Road is still standing, but is in a sorry state, and has been identified for demolition. The profile of this iconic building will be missed, both from the roadside and from the canal side, where its distinctive façade provides a navigational aid for holidaymakers, walkers and working boatpeople.

30. Great Central Railway (GCR), 1898

Loughborough, being in the centre of England, has always had good transport links – canals, railways and motorways – which, being such an important part of Sir Edward Watkins' plan for a rail link between Yorkshire and Lancashire connected to mainland Europe via a channel tunnel in the mid-1850s, helped to ensure Loughborough was well connected.

The GCR was named in 1897 when the Manchester, Sheffield & Lincolnshire Railway (MS&LR) changed its name to reflect the imminent opening of its extension line to

London, work which began in 1894 and was completed by 1898. The MS&LR had itself been formed in 1847 by the merger of several railway companies. The route ran across the Pennines, via the East Midlands including Loughborough, and on to London Marylebone. The London extension was the last major main line to be built in the UK.

Until the Railways Act 1921 came into force in 1923, there existed nine major railway companies in England, of which the GCR was one. With the implementation of the Act, nine became the Big Four, the GCR becoming part of the London & North-Eastern Railway (LNER). When nationalisation came in 1948, GCR became part of the Eastern Railways, before being transferred to the Midland region of British Railways in 1958. The Midland Railway had always viewed the GCR as a competitor, and so began the decline of the GCR. Eventually, in 1966, most of the line was closed, Loughborough station closing in 1969.

Designed by Edward Parry, the Loughborough station building was completed in 1898, being reopened in 1974, and the Great Central Railway (GCR), a private company created in 1976. Other stations along the line between Loughborough and Leicester North were also reopened. Today, the booking hall still has its beautiful wood-panelled walls, and the stairway down to the platforms still has its luggage slide on the side. It has been said that the platform canopy is the largest on any preserved railway.

As the UK's only double-track main line heritage railway, the GCR is a very popular attraction. Special events are well attended and trains run every weekend of the year and at various other times. There are also exquisite dining opportunities, the chance to drive a steam locomotive and a dedicated museum at Loughborough station.

There are plans to reconnect the line between Loughborough and South Nottingham, which will open up an 18-mile stretch of track.

Looking onto one of the GCR platforms.

Above: The grand entrance to the GCR.

Below: The entrance to the GCR showing signals, a wall-mounted post box, the glass canopy and date stones.

31. Charnwood Museum, 1898

In celebration of the first diamond jubilee of a British monarch, towns honoured Queen Victoria in a myriad of ways. In Loughborough, talks started and plans began to be formed in 1894 for creating a park in the centre of town, where local people could take advantage of walking in the fresh air, and public bathing.

Mr F. R. Griggs contributed to the park by selling land that belonged to Island House, the public contributed to the cost of creating the park, and Joseph Griggs, the first mayor of the borough of Loughborough, contributed to the cost of the baths, the eventual cost of which were £4,000.

Opened in 1898, the Memorial Baths, designed by G. H. Barrowcliff at the same time as he was working on the bell foundry with E. H. Allcock, was built of local red brick and embellished with terracotta. The baths contained therein were 80 feet long and 30 feet wide, and were surrounded by thirty dressing rooms, nine slipper baths, comprising four first-class and five second-class baths, a laundry and offices. The official opening ceremony for the park and the baths was held in 1899.

The baths proved very popular, and chlorination was introduced in 1934. However, by 1975 a new leisure centre had opened nearby, and increasing problems with maintaining the water quality in the Memorial Baths led to their closing. Renamed the Queen's Hall, in 1980 the hall became a venue for a variety of one-off events like craft fairs, and for the weekly bric-a-brac market.

Charnwood Museum, Queen's Park.

In 1998 the building was further transformed into Charnwood Museum, which officially opened in 1999. The museum consists of permanent displays of artefacts central to the history and development of Loughborough and the Charnwood area, as well as a number of regularly changing exhibition cases and galleries.

Left: Detail of the Charnwood Museum building.

Below: View of Charnwood Museum from the Great Paul bell casing.

32. Pizza Express, 1900

This magnificent building has recently been rescued, renovated and given a new lease of life. The building has been Grade II listed since 1984, and, despite a variety of occupants, sometime around 2008 it was abandoned and disintegrating, with shards of brick regularly breaking off and landing on the pavement.

Built around the turn of the century, it originally housed an auction mart, Garton and Amatt. Typical of the late nineteenth-century auction marts, this building had an elaborate street frontage and extensive rooms behind, which would have been used for viewing and storing items and for holding sales. Upstairs was at one time a dining room. Also typical of auction marts of the era, No. 54 Baxter Gate had a small carriageway arch to the left of the frontage, adjacent to No. 53.

The Art and Crafts design was popular at the time of construction, and the brick building is enhanced with the use of terracotta and tiling. Also of note are the oriel windows in the attic and the octagonal turret.

When Garton and Amatt vacated the premises, the building became associated with the hospital next door. Over the years, No. 54 has been the nurses' home, a doctor's surgery and a health information centre.

The hospital, built in 1862 and extended in 1931, was abandoned when a new hospital opened on Epinal Way, and like No. 54 it lay empty for a number of years, until being demolished in 2011. The future of No. 54 hung in the balance. Luckily, there was a major redevelopment plan for the old hospital site, and the renovation of No. 54 was pivotal to this.

The successful work done by Pizza Express has breathed new life into this beautiful building and preserved it for many generations to come.

Disintegrating in 2013.

Above: Rescued in 2016.

Below: Reinvigorated in 2017.

33. Temperance Hall, 1900

The foundation stone for the Temperance Hall was laid by the mayor of Sheffield in 1899, following four years of fundraising activities by folk committed to creating a dedicated meeting place for the Loughborough branch of the Temperance Society. Some townspeople had been strong supporters of the temperance movement since as early as 1840, when Loughborough was the destination chosen by Thomas Cook (of holiday company fame) for his temperance outing from Leicester on the newly built Midland railway.

Built on the corner of Granby Street and Cattle Market, the Temperance Hall was designed by the local architect A. E. King, who made good use of the awkwardly shaped plot. The bricks were made by the local firm of Tucker's and the woodwork by the local firm of Corah. Unexpectedly, however, the terracotta was not created by the local Hathern Station Brick and Terra Cotta Co., but by J. C. Edwards of Wales.

With a café at one end and a public hall at the other, the building also housed a first- and second-class dining room, a separate room for ladies, a small hall with a committee room and a large kitchen. At 57 feet by 31 feet 6 inches, the large hall had a capacity of 500, having a gallery at one end with side rooms off and a billiard room at the back.

The mayor of Sheffield commented on the proximity of several licensed premises (maybe The Old Boot, The Volunteer, and the Golden Fleece) and congratulated society members on their courage in choosing such a site for their meeting hall!

Temperance Hall viewed from Granby Street.

Temperance Hall viewed from Cattle Market.

While the Temperance Hall, the building was also a venue for parties and dances, and in 1909 a permanent film projection box was added. When the Empire Cinema was built, films continued to be shown at the hall, but the coming of the Victory Cinema in 1921 proved too much competition and the Temperance Hall became the Palais de Danse, before being sold to Garton's the local auction mart.

Garton's vacated the building in the early twenty-first century, and the ground floor is now occupied by a betting shop and the upstairs is used by an aikido club.

34. Public Library, 1905

A competition to design a new library resulted in an Edwardian baroque-style public library building. This replaced the 1886 library on the corner of Green Close Lane, which was considered no longer adequate. The Scottish-Anglo industrialist and philanthropist Andrew Carnegie had pledged £5,000 towards its building, as had local man Griggs, and it was prominent and prolific local architects Barrowcliff and Allcock who won the design competition.

One of the assessors of the competition entries was George Hodson. As founder of the Hathern Station Brick and Terra Cotta Co., it comes as no surprise that the resulting library building has much terracotta detailing. The bricks were made by the local firm of Tucker's, and the builders were the local firm of Moss, both of whom would later be involved with the construction of the Carillon. The heating system was installed by the local firm Messengers.

When originally built, the main entrance to the library was to the side of the reading room, but this was removed in the 1960s when the extension was constructed, the latter being on land freed up by the demolition of nearby Island House, which was adjacent to the library. At the rear of the building, facing onto Packe Street, was – and still is – the librarian's house, which included a corridor linking it directly to the library.

Over the years the internal layout of the library has changed many times to make best use of technological advances, and most recently, in 2013, the library underwent a major refurbishment resulting in a bright, welcoming space for the many customers and groups who use the library. Lower shelving on castors also means the library can create different spaces to host a variety of events.

The best view of this Carnegie public library is from the exit of Queen's Park onto Granby Street.

Librarian's house at the rear of the library.

Public library viewed from Granby Street.

Public library viewed in the distance from Queen's Park.

35. Denhams, 1907

The building that houses Denhams the Jewellers is a magnificent example of an Arts and Crafts design, built in 1907.

The impressive square tower on the corner of High Street and Baxter Gate, as well as the upper floors, are faced in buff terracotta tiles, most probably made by the Hathern Station Brick and Terra Cotta Co. An egg and dart frieze flows around the top of the first-floor windows, and the swags and tails over the arched corner doorway are painted on a gold-coloured background.

In its early years, the premises were used by G. H. Miller, jewellers, but by 1951 Millers had become a costumier. A local trade directory for 1962 shows that Denhams the Jewellers were operating from the shop, and continued to do so until 2015 when the family-run business was taken over by jewellers Francis & Gaye.

Right: The square tower and arched doorway.

Below: Denhams extends along Baxter Gate.

36. Lloyds Bank, 1907

Sitting proudly on the corner of Loughborough High Street at its junction with the pedestrianised Market Place and built on the site of the former Consumers' Tea Company, the Lloyds Bank occupies a locally listed building.

Constructed in the early twentieth century, this building is a typical example of a turn-of-the-twentieth-century bank building: its proportions are generous, its position ideal and its decoration exquisite. The curved forms of the bas-reliefs that adorn the building between the first- and second-floor windows are typical of the Art Nouveau style, as are the beautifully carved fish swimming around on the parapet.

An allegorical, high relief figure sits majestically atop the parapet between fish and urns, holding in the right hand a rolled-up deed or scroll and in the left a money bag. Sadly, over the last fifteen years, there has been major deterioration and the figure has lost the left hand at the elbow, and there are some pretty, but inappropriate yellow flowers blossoming from the first-floor-level string course.

Although the architect has not been identified, a comparison with the Nottingham and Nottinghamshire Banking Company Bank in the Bullring, Shepshed (now Charnwood Dental Centre) – which is also highly embellished – indicates a possibility that Lloyds Bank in Loughborough was designed by A. E. King, and likely embellished by George Harry Cox, more of whose work can be seen in Loughborough Market Place.

Good use is made of local materials and local skills: the bank was constructed by local builders, Moss, and the terracotta used in the embellishments and decoration was produced by the Hathern Station Brick and Terra Cotta Co.

Originally, the main entrance to the bank was situated directly at the junction of High Street and Market Place, but during the 1980s this was moved to the High Street side of the building, and an extension to the bank was built on the Market Place site vacated by the demolished Blackamoors Head pub on High Street. More recently, the entrance has returned to its original position, making for a much grander entrance.

The exquisite parapet decoration of Lloyds Bank.

The reinstated corner entrance on the far right.

37. The Odeon, 1914/1936

The Empire opened in 1914, and was the first purpose-built cine-variety house in Loughborough. Thomas Mayo, mayor of Loughborough at the time, opened the venue on Monday 14 September, the first advert appearing in the *Loughborough Echo* of 11 September.

As a cine-variety house, the Empire showed silent films, accompanied by an orchestra, and also included variety turns. The talkies arrived in 1929, and the building façade was rebuilt, with two gable ends fronting onto what was then Market Place, which is today known as Cattle Market. However, it wasn't until 1931 that a new sound system was installed.

The Empire, the Victory Cinema, and the Theatre Royal were owned by Percy Oswin, and in 1933 he sold them to Charles K. Deeming, a local man who already owned cinemas in nearby Coalville. When, in 1936, the state-of-the-art Odeon was built, Deeming decided to upgrade the Empire, and a new auditorium was built behind the current Empire. In order to not lose custom, the Empire did not close during the renovation work for a temporary entrance was made on Wood Gate, allowing the original cinema to be gutted, while cinemagoers could still be entertained. When it was completed, there was a new entrance with a café downstairs and a restaurant and ballroom upstairs.

What resulted from this 1936 renovation was the striking art deco façade, which still graces Cattle Market today. Constructed from cream Hathernware (formerly Hathern Station Brick and Terra Cotta Co.) tiles, with a central turret, the parapets are dressed in glazed blue copings atop a typically art deco-themed decorative frieze.

In 1952, Deeming sold his two cinemas to Essoldo, and the Empire went through a period of quick name-changes – the Essoldo in 1953, the Curzon in 1954, the Classic in 1967, back to the Curzon in 1974, the Reel in 1999 – and eventually became part of the Odeon chain in 2011. Since 1952 extra screens have been added, now making a total of six.

Today competition for the Odeon comes from the recently built Cineworld multiplex cinema on Baxter Gate, next to Pizza Express.

Art deco façade, 2018.

Right: The Curzon with six films on show.

Below: The tower from the rear.

Art deco side windows.

38. Loughborough Carillon Tower and War Memorial Museum, 1922–23

Queen's Park is the perfect setting for Loughborough's unusual war memorial. The Grade II-listed Carillon Tower, built following public consultation, provides a lasting memorial to local people who perished in the First World War. Heanor chose a memorial hospital, Quorn a memorial garden, other towns a stained-glass church window, or other monuments, but Loughborough chose to honour its dead by building a towering structure housing a carillon. The bells would be reminiscent of those more commonly found in Belgium; many of those to whom the Carillon is dedicated, fell at Ypres.

Walter Tapper, the architect appointed to design the edifice, was a contemporary of Sir George Gilbert Scott, and most noted for his churches. In the latter part of his career Tapper was president of the Royal Institute of British Architects.

The construction of the tower was a most local affair: built by Moss with bricks by Tucker's, steelwork by Herbert Morris and the bells of the carillon made by Taylors Bell Founders.

A Portland stone base and window dressing, with pointing of Portland cement, complement the local materials. At 151 feet tall, the tower weighs a total of 1,300 tons. The main gallery projecting from the body of the tower is surrounded by sixteen columns that support the roof, and an octagonal gallery with a turret, topped by a cupola roof, rises from this gallery. Access is through the large wooden doors at ground level, then via the spiral stone stairs.

The foundation stones were laid in 1922 by General Lord Horne and Mrs J. T. Godber, and the memorial was unveiled by Field Marshal Sir William Robertson on Sunday 22 July 1923. In 1928, a stone balustrade around the base of the tower was added, and in 1981 floodlighting was presented by the descendants of the Tucker family.

Today, the tower contains the Leicestershire Yeomanry museum, and items related to the American 82nd Airborne Division, 505th Parachute Infantry Regiment, who were stationed at Quorn in 1944. Regular Carillon recitals are given by the Carilloneur and each November, the Carillon is the focus for the annual Service of Remembrance.

Above left: Paper poppies falling from the Carillon in November 2016.

Above right: The Carillon in autumn.

Below: The Carillon in winter 2017.

39. Poundstretcher, 1930

One could be forgiven for walking past this High Street shop without a second glance, or perhaps with a thought that the vivid red plastic shop fascia and the large window panes are unattractive. However, approaching High Street from Baxter Gate gives a perfect opportunity to look up and observe the magnificence of this building, quite different in styling from many of the other art deco buildings in the town, as it also harks back to the Domestic Revival style.

Replacing a tailor, a butcher and a hatter, the new shop, opened in 1930, was home to Russell Smith & Co., drapers. The business already traded from a substantial retail space on the opposite side of High Street, at Nos 4, 5 and 5a, which opened in 1914, but the range of goods available had gradually expanded and extra premises were needed. The new store had two small shop windows at ground floor level, on either side of a central bay, and under this bay was a walkaround window display. A beautiful black and white tiled floor led customers into the store.

By 1939 Russell Smith, drapers, had given up Nos 5 and 5a High Street and were trading only from No. 4 and the 1930 building opposite. This continued until well into the latter half of the twentieth century, with Russell Smith maintaining stores on both sides of High Street. An advert appearing in a local street directory in 1962 describes the business as 'Russell Smith & Co. Drapers and Furriers, High Street (both sides) Loughboro' and

Russell Smith & Co. in 2017.

Detail of Russell Smith & Co.

the alphabetical entry qualifies that this is specifically a "ladies" outfitters, drapers and furriers'. Reflecting the growth of the population and telephone ownership, the telephone number has changed from 152 in 1928 to 2152 in 1962.

In the late twentieth century the building was modernised, and the windows extended across most of the frontage. The ground-floor showroom has also been completely remodelled, but the grand sweeping staircase still provides access to the first floor.

4c. Blacksmith's Arms, 1931

Built in 1931, the Blacksmith's Arms in Ward's End replaced an earlier pub building also called the Blacksmith's Arms, although prior to 1875 the pub had been called The Blackboy.

It is quite common for pubs to be named for a specific reason, but the origin of the name Blackboy has never been proven, despite it being a popular name across the country for many years. Theories are that it might relate to the commemoration of Charles II in some way, or perhaps there is some connection with the slave trade, or maybe the name is related to the trade of chimney sweeps or coal miners.

There is, however, no doubt that the Blacksmith's Arms is named after the trade of the landlord who was the licensee at the time of the name change, for Luke Birkin was indeed a blacksmith, and in 1875 when he changed the name of the pub, it was common for publicans to run a pub alongside their main trade or craft.

During the late 1920s/early 1930s, many town buildings were demolished to enable the roads to be widened. Most of this took place at the other end of town along Market Street, High Street, Baxter Gate and Swan Street, but clearly there was some redevelopment in the Ward's End area. The Blacksmith's Arms (along with The Swan in the Rushes) is a wonderful example of an art deco building, stripped neoclassical in style, half red brick (now hidden under black paint) and half what are most probably tiles made by Hathernware.

In recent years the pub has changed name and function a number of times – Smiths, @The Office, VooDoo, Liquid Spice, Baroque – but is currently trading as a pub called The Blacksmiths.

Above: The Blacksmiths in 2017.

Left: Detail of the art deco windows.

41. *Echo* Offices, 1931

The street widening of Loughborough in the late 1920s/early 1930s offered an opportunity to demolish rather dilapidated buildings and replace them with buildings of a more current design. This era in the arts is characterised by the art deco movement, and the former *Echo Press* offices is a striking example of this style, although there are many other buildings in the town centre and further afield that are equally impressive.

Common features of these art deco buildings in Loughborough is the use of cream faience tiles, created by Hathernware. The *Echo* building was designed by the local architect E. J. Allcock, and the specific features that make this design a little different from that of

Right: The colourful Egyptianate columns.

Below: The *Loughborough Echo* building.

similar buildings (for example, the Delice café on Baxter Gate) are the *Echo Press* logo atop the pediment, and the beautifully fashioned and coloured Egyptian-ate columns, which are now sadly surrounded by crude square wooden protection.

Next to the *Echo Press* logo is the date 1891, which is when the *Echo Press* was established, its previous location being on Dead Lane. These new premises contained

The *Echo Press* logo.

editorial offices on the ground floor, with a shop selling fancy goods and stationery, and where adverts could be brought. The general offices were upstairs. Clearly the *Echo Press* were proud of their new offices as in a 1932 issue of the *Loughborough Echo*, the journalist says the buildings are modern, yet dignified, and a valuable contribution to the architectural amenities of the town.

Today the *Loughborough Echo* continues to provide townsfolk with local news in a weekly newspaper, and the *Echo Press* offices are on a nearby industrial estate.

42. Bastard Gates, 1933

Built on the north-east corner of the Loughborough University campus in close proximity to the former halls of residence Hazlerigg and Rutland – affectionately known as Rigg-Rut – the Bastard Gates were opened in 1934, and originally served as the main entrance to the university playing fields from Ashby Road.

The naming of this entrance often causes amusement among the university's students, but this belies the serious nature of the gift of the gates, made by William Bastard, after whom they are named. When Rutland Hall was officially opened in 1932, Herbert Schofield, the principal of what was then Loughborough College, declared that William Bastard, chairman of the college governors from 1934 to 1936, was donating the flamboyant entrance arch to the college.

In 2016–17 the gates underwent a programme of restoration, and today the crest and shield on either side of the crown of the arch stand out beautifully clear and proud, showing a shared history between town and gown.

Above: Bastard Gates entrance to the university.

Below: The refurbished stonework.

43. Beacon Bingo, 1936

Opened in 1936 as an Odeon Cinema for the Oscar Deutsch chain on the site of the former general post office, this stunning building is a typical example of Odeon cinemas, being constructed in the Streamlined Modernist style. Deutsch opened his first UK cinema in Brierley Hill, Staffordshire, in 1928, and the first of the Odeon chain in 1930 in Perry Barr.

The Loughborough Odeon, designed by the architects Arthur J. Price and Harry Weedon, who were designers of many Odeon cinemas, provided seating for over 1,600 cinemagoers, and was one of twenty-eight purpose-built Odeon cinemas opened around the country in 1936. The opening show that November was Columbia Pictures' *Mr Deeds Goes to Town*, a romantic comedy directed by Frank Capra and starring Gary Cooper and Jean Arthur. In 2016 Stuart Maconie, on recreating the Jarrow March of 1936, recognised what a striking building this would have been – and still is!

Loughborough town centre already had two cinemas – the Empire, opened in 1914, and the Victory, opened in 1921 – but since film production in the UK was then at an all-time high, and the 'golden age' of Hollywood stretched from the late 1920s to the early 1960s, there was a strong enough demand from the cinemagoing public to sustain all three.

Like many other buildings in the town, local building and decorative material was used and provides a striking exterior for the Loughborough Odeon. This was a showcase building for Hathernware, whose biscuit-coloured faience tiles, unusually in a basket weave

The former Odeon, now Beacon Bingo.

Hathernware partnered with red brick.

pattern and with black and green banding across the top, adorn the area rising above the entrance level, while the base is similarly dressed in black tiles with green banding. The Loughborough Odeon has an unusual brick poster frame along part of its length on the Lemyngton Street side.

The Odeon Loughborough was sold to the Classic Cinema chain in 1967, ironically the same year that the Victory was demolished, but its popularity waned until it finally closed as a cinema in 1974, first becoming a Mecca bingo club, and now flourishing as a branch of the Beacon Bingo chain.

44. Towers Hall of Residence, 1964–67

Loughborough University campus comprises a variety of buildings in a diverse range of styles, reflecting the development of the institution over a number of years. From the 1920s the campus was home to Loughborough College of Education, and this period saw much building work to provide both teaching and residential accommodation for its students. Rutland Hall was opened in 1932, Victory Sports Hall in 1946, and the Music Block and College Library came shortly after. A further dedicated hall of residence soon followed.

The Towers is a landmark that can be seen from far and wide, and was constructed in the 1960s as living accommodation for students of the college. It was designed by the architectural firm of Gollins, Melvin and Ward (GMW), who had very recently designed Sheffield University Library, which today is a Grade II-listed building. GMW were also responsible for the design of Marathon House (formerly Castrol House), London, featuring an early use of architectural curtain walling.

Above: Towers viewed from the Charnwood hills.

Left: Towers among construction work.

Constructed by local building company Moss, work on the Towers began in 1964 and was completed by 1967. As with many buildings of the era, Towers was built using steel reinforced concrete – a massive 1,180 tons of concrete, moulded around a web of steel. The pour of concrete is believed to be one of the largest to take place in the Midlands, and used a relay of twenty-two lorries, taking nine hours to complete the job.

There are two towers, East Tower being sixteen floors high, West Tower twenty-one, with a central lift shaft and stairs. East Tower consists of six individual study rooms, one bathroom and one kitchen, while West Tower has eleven study rooms and two bathrooms and kitchens. Although the study rooms are a non-conventional shape (some might even suggest they are coffin-like), students are enticed by their Student Union to reside in 'the tallest hall … [with] refurbished rooms, which are one of the biggest on campus … and a view that would make the owner of the Shard jealous'. Towers is as popular today as it has always been.

45. John Storer House, 1966

At the head of Ward's End stands John Storer House (JSH), a building that is very typical of the style so popular in Britain in the 1960s, although these are not abundant in Loughborough town centre – a further example is the extension to the public library.

JSH is a community centre and the headquarters for Voluntary Action Charnwood, as well as a meeting place for a wide variety of groups including a bridge club and the Macular Disease Society, and home to services like the Youth Probation Service.

John Storer House.

The centre is part of John Storer Charnwood (JSC), a charitable organisation concerned with the promotion of community activity and community well-being through varied services, programmes, events and café offering.

JSC originated around 1713 when John Storer, a man about whom little is known, founded a charity, transferring land and dwellings in Loughborough to a group of trustees. Bread was made from the wheat purchased with the income from the charity and given to the poor of Loughborough. In 1891, it was decided to change the focus of the charitable work: half the income would be used for poor relief and half for the education of local children, although the provision of clothing, which was part of the original charity work, continued until 1899.

JSH itself came about when, after consideration and consultation, the trust, which was looking at ways to use the income from the sale of parcels of land, which culminated in the early 1960s, agreed to provide a day centre for the elderly on a site formerly occupied by the Emmanuel Boys' School. Some funds were provided by the county council, and further money was raised during a week of special events, to cover the estimated building costs of £40,000. On 29 April 1966 John Storer House was officially opened by the Princess Margaret.

Today, JSH has a refurbished café, a shop selling locally made products and a thriving community of users. In 2016, JSH celebrated its fiftieth birthday and is now looking for funding to renovate its windows. JSH also takes an active part in the Loughborough 'In Bloom' competition.

JSH 'In Bloom'.

46. Ladybird, 1971

Near the Great Central Railway on Beeches Road stands a modest 1970s building, home to the Anstey Wallpaper Co., called Ladybird House, an interesting name and one that hints at a history.

Henry Wills had been a printer and a retailer of stationery and books in Loughborough Market Place since as early as 1867, producing local street directories, seed catalogues and posters. In 1904, William Hepworth joined Wills in the business, and trade was plentiful until the outbreak of the First World War, when printing work dwindled. A decision to produce a children's book in 1915 completely changed the direction of the company and led to its longevity at a time when other printers in the town were closing or moving.

At the time, Market Place consisted of a market area lined with shops, at the side of many were alleyways leading to yards behind, and it was from Angel Yard that Wills and Hepworth operated their business. The first children's book they produced was issued by the Angel Press, but in 1915 they registered the Ladybird logo. The familiar format of Ladybird books emerged in the 1940s, by which time Henry Wills had left the company, and in the 1970s the publishing name changed from Wills and Hepworth to Ladybird Books.

In 1971 the company was taken over by Pearson Publishing, who also owned Penguin Books, and the publishing operation moved to purpose-built premises on Beeches Road. Ladybird Books continued to be hugely successful, and in 1998 the company was merged with Penguin, work transferring from the Loughborough factory to London. Ladybird Books are still published today, and collecting older editions has become a popular hobby and business.

Ladybird House, once home of Ladybird Books and now to Anstey Wallpaper Co.

Rear of Ladybird House viewed from the GCR.

The Anstey Wallpaper Co. relocated its business to Ladybird House in 1999 and is now named after the village where its business began. The company uses a variety of printing techniques to produce its wallcoverings, including surface printing, traditional block printing and screen printing, as well as the latest digital printing techniques. The company professes to be the only wallcovering factory that uses every possible printing process under one roof.

47. Swimming Pool, Loughborough University, 2002

Until as late as 1986, Loughborough University campus offered three swimming pools: a small, covered affair close to the Edward Herbert Building (EHB), an outdoor pool close to Victory Hall, and one inside it. Today, the university boasts a magnificent 50-metre Olympic-sized pool gracing the grassy bank adjacent to Epinal Way, the ring road around the town.

Built in 2002 at a cost of £6 million, the pool was state of the art, providing eight lanes with a maximum depth of 2 meters. The English Swimming Squad, who took part in the Commonwealth Games of 2002, were some of the first users of the pool, and since then it has been the training venue for elite athletes.

A boom running through the centre of the pool can divide the pool into two 25-meter pools. Swimming lessons are provided for children; the floor of the pool is moveable, raising this makes the depth of the water shallower, better suited to children's needs. The pool is also available to members of the local community for recreational purposes, and various events are hosted throughout the year.

The flower display between the pool and Epinal Way is always well tended and topical, and no doubt contributes to success in the 'In Bloom' competition.

Swimming pool and flower display viewed from Epinal Way.

48. Magistrates' Court, 2007

The new award-winning Magistrates' Court in Loughborough was built and opened in 2007. Designed by Stephen George & Partners, in conjunction with Wilmott Dixon, and costing £15 million, the new court replaced the former Magistrates' Court on Wood Gate.

The Wood Gate court, which originally housed the police station, opened on 27th September 1860, but when in 1975 the police service moved to a new building off Southfield Road (which has itself been replaced in 2015) the building became solely the Magistrates' Court. Initially, there were two courtrooms, later increasing to four, a large room on the ground floor where fines would have been paid, and underneath the main courtroom were three cells, with small windows at pavement level.

Once the new court was built, the old courthouse transferred to the care of the local authority, and it is now home to the Workers Educational Association, a café and other charitable groups. The location of the new courthouse is nearby, but when originally built access was quite limited, and it was situated next to a small scruffy car park, which in turn was adjacent to the NHS walk-in centre. The walk-in centre was built near the site of the former William Cotton's hosiery machine works on Pinfold Gate, which backed up to the former General Hospital whose entrance was on Baxter Gate. When plans for the Inner Relief road were released, and the road eventually constructed, the position of the new Magistrates' Court was immediately changed, making it a roadside feature with wide pavements and parking to the rear.

The striking new courthouse, faced in cream stone with tinted glass, was the winner of the Leicester and Rutland Society of Architects Design Award in March 2009.

Above: The Wood Gate court.

Below: The award-winning Magistrates' Court.

49. Devonshire Square Mural, 2014

On Tuesday 26 January 1965, Councillor G. J. Humphrey, mayor of the borough of Loughborough, officially opened a two-storey car park on Granby Street in the presence of aldermen and former mayors William P. Stagg, L. W. Hull and George G. Allen and Councillor Mrs M. Bradley. Alderman Stagg pleaded with motorists to make use of the new car park instead of 'cluttering up the streets'.

The new car park was originally intended to be four storeys, but at the time of opening it was a two-deck construction, although sufficiently load-bearing to take the two extra levels that had been planned. The entrance was on Granby Street, but the length of the structure faced onto Devonshire Square and the ground level was populated by shops.

What the car park had replaced was Clarke's Dye Works, a long-established family firm that was liquidated in 1959, with the building demolished not long after.

The car park lasted for many years until around 2012 when the upper levels were removed, and the ground-level rear parking area was spruced up. Following the town's acceptance as a second wave Mary Portas Pilot town, a plan for revitalising the Devonshire Square area was suggested, and Wei Ong, who calls himself Silent Hobo, was chosen from a group of twenty artists to create an exciting mural to cover the railings that remained above the shops. Wei Ong had created much artwork for other towns, and after consultation with local residents, he planned his Loughborough mural to showcase some of the town's heritage, its seasonal events and its local people.

On Sunday 7 December 2014, the unveiling of Wei Ong's mural was attended by many people, which has remained a talking point to this day.

Mural showing the Carillon to the far right.

In 2017 during the annual November fair.

50. Bridge to the Future, 2017

The early hours of Sunday 3 September 2017 proved to be exciting as steam railway enthusiasts lined the Nottingham Road railway bridge over the Midland Main Line to watch a momentous event. A few days earlier a 1,000-tonne crane had been installed in the vicinity, and on the night in question it reared into action, ready for the Big Lift.

Since the closure of the Great Central Railway line to London in 1966 (Loughborough station closing in 1969), and the formation of the Great Central Railway (1976) Ltd, volunteers have worked tirelessly to bring steam trains back to the area and to provide an exciting experience for visitors. The double track between Loughborough and Rothley was reinstated, and a new station, Leicester North, built at Birstall.

A further major aim of the volunteers is to reinstate the line between Loughborough and South Nottingham, making an exciting journey of 18 miles possible. In order to achieve this, bridges need to be reinstalled and embankments rebuilt.

One of these bridges, spanning the Midland Main Line just south of Loughborough railway station – called the 'Bridge to the Future' – was hauled into place on that warm September night, a huge task that took nearly three hours to complete. The next stage of the project is 'Crossing the Canal', which involves repairs to one of the canal bridges. With every stage we are closer to making future history.

Above: The crane in position, September 2017.

Below: The bridge in place.

Above: A Midland Main Line train passes under the newly installed bridge.

Below: The GCR – Bridge to the Future!